INSIDE THE MIND

Edited By Lynsey Evans

First published in Great Britain in 2025 by:

Young Writers
Remus House
Coltsfoot Drive
Peterborough
PE2 9BF
Telephone: 01733 890066
Website: www.youngwriters.co.uk

All Rights Reserved
Book Design by Ashley Janson
© Copyright Contributors 2024
Softback ISBN 978-1-83685-151-6
Printed and bound in the UK by BookPrintingUK
Website: www.bookprintinguk.com
YB0624V

Foreword

Since 1991, here at Young Writers we have celebrated the awesome power of creative writing, especially in young adults where it can serve as a vital method of expressing their emotions and views about the world around them. In every poem we see the effort and thought that each student published in this book has put into their work and by creating this anthology we hope to encourage them further with the ultimate goal of sparking a life-long love of writing.

Our latest competition for secondary school students, The Beautiful Truth, asked young writers to consider what their truth is, what's important to them, and how to express that using the power of words. We wanted to give them a voice, the chance to express themselves freely and honestly, something which is so important for these young adults to feel confident and listened to. They could give an opinion, highlight an issue, consider a dilemma, impart advice or simply write about something they love. There were no restrictions on style or subject so you will find an anthology brimming with a variety of poetic styles and topics. We hope you find it as absorbing as we have.

We encourage young writers to express themselves and address subjects that matter to them, which sometimes means writing about sensitive or contentious topics. If you have been affected by any issues raised in this book, details on where to find help can be found at
www.youngwriters.co.uk/info/other/contact-lines

Contents

Bungay High School, Bungay

Isabelle Fennelly (11)	1
Oliver Hall (12)	2
Angelyn Johny (12)	4
Mia Macfarlane (13)	6
Ryan Page (11)	7

Macmillan Academy, Middlesbrough

Blossom Uzoigwe (15)	8
Fridaus Juma (13)	11
Alexis Jaques (12)	12
Aisha Hussain (12)	13
Faith Williams (12)	14
Imogen Stockton (14)	16
Lorelei Myers (13)	17
Skye Mockett (12)	18
Deborah Oshode (12)	19
Martha Towers (14)	20
Sian Large (12)	21
Esther Golden (12)	22
Tyler Saunders (12)	23

Magna Academy, Canford Heath

Tolu Opesanwo (13)	24
Milo Buck (13)	26
Noah Clinton (13)	28
Ty'ron Bello (13)	30
Max Simpson (12)	31
Lucas Cornachini Paiva	32
Harry Lawrence (12)	34
Quinn Rickard-Muller (13)	36
Mirela Manea (14)	38
Danni Popa (13)	39

Anabelle Harris (12)	40
Zara Hausawi (12)	41
Jack Parsons (12)	42
Rubie Burt (13)	44
Cohen Rutt (12)	45
Zac Wilson (13)	46
Renesmee Bennett (13)	47
Zoe Fox (12)	48
Ryan Earl (13)	50
Nade Hawkins (13)	51
Nataliia Sokol (12)	52
Ben Sims (13)	53
Sophia Epton (13)	54
Emma Caseley (14)	55
Rodin Turan (13)	56
Oliver Malone (14)	57
Amelia Conroy (13)	58
Leo Waddington (12)	59
Jessica Miller (12)	60
Lewis Ashdown (13)	61
Oliver Stevenson (13)	62
Daisy Hall (13)	63
Jakub Labik (13)	64
Oscar Stockley-King (13)	65
Libbie Gurd (12)	66
Maya-Louise Rammell (13)	67
Karabo Baitshoki (13)	68
Max Richardson (12)	69
Mason Urbanski (13)	70
Noah-Kythe Hemnebelle (13)	71
Callum Bourton (12)	72
Shyanne Taylor (13)	73
Robert Heed (13)	74
Humaid Hussain (12)	75
Baylee Pittam (12)	76

Miyah Elizabeth-Skye Mangan (13)	77
Millie Brown (13)	78
Briley Hayward (12)	79
Athena Shukry (13)	80
Lucy Moutray (12)	81
Dylan Wilson (12)	82
Bella Churchill (13)	83
Leonardo Cornachini Paiva (13)	84
Lilie Walters (13)	85
Oliver Nippard (13)	86
William P Roberts (12)	87
Hope Hatchard (13)	88
Julia Chudek (12)	89
Leon Bailey (12)	90
Lexi Roberts (13)	91
Eva Martin (12)	92
Ometh Samarasekara (13)	93
Ethan King (13)	94
Charlie Fitzgerald (13)	95
Sophia Pritchard (13)	96
Ella Vincent (12)	97
Ometh Samarsekara (13)	98
Paige Robins (13)	99
Lewis Hill (12)	100
Ollie Schofield (13)	101
Mia-Lilly Pill (12)	102
Aaron Hill (12)	103

Matravers School, Westbury

Poppy Stott (11)	104
Holly Butcher (14)	106
Georgia Scott (11)	107
Lev Dzisiak (13)	108

Pedmore High School, Stourbridge

Hadia Kawal	109
Rebeka Jurek	110
Ethan Cox	112
Deen Ahmed (12)	113
Alvy Lawerence (13)	114
Eva Brazier (11)	116
Aadam Khan (12)	118

Maddison Bowen (11)	119
Mya Fleming	120
Umar Ahmed (12)	121
Sami Abbas (14)	122
Vuyisile Bango (14)	123
Jessica-Mai	124
Kimberley Moroua	125
Molly Wheelwright	126
Benjamin Hunt	127
Marcy Cheslin	128
Ethan Munjunju	129
Chloe Leonard	130
Thomas Bunting (13)	131
Sophia Coleiro (13)	132
Amie-Lou Owers	133
Amina Bashyer	134
Kaiya Hoskins (13)	135
Thayne (11)	136
Shourouk Haj Ibrahim (11)	137
Muhammad Yusuf Ali-Usman (11)	138
Hidayah Ilyas	139
Jack Davis (12)	140
Lilly Skelding (13)	141
Lily-Ann Mills (14)	142
Lacey Price-Adkins	143
Joshua Hedworth (14)	144
Grace Peters (12)	145
Eduard Baloi (12)	146
Eddie Lewis Bladen	147
Daniel Davis (14)	148
Isabella Davies (12)	149
Theo Darnley (11)	150
Coralie Jones (12)	151
Scarlett Homer (11)	152
Anastasia Archer-Smith	153
Saif Asghar (12)	154
Kai Toogood	155
Natalia Fetita (13)	156
Tuliyah-Jae Sutton	157
Imogen Harris (11)	158
Aisha Ahmed (12)	159

Penglais School, Aberystwyth

Eve Tiddeman (12)	160
Rhiannon Starr (11)	162
Tilly Greenhalgh-Donnai (11)	163
Nancy Sophia Gorman (12)	164
Jewel Mathew (14)	165
Gabriel Brown (11)	166
Lily Potts (11)	167

THE POEMS

FREEDOM
BELIEVE!
HONESTY
TRUTH

The Dinosaur And The Asteroid

D inosaurs roamed the world years ago,
I guanodon, stegosaurus, carnosaurs, and many others.
N o dino knew about the asteroid ready to blow,
O nly one egg survived. Asteroids hit dinos and their mothers,
S oaring through the sky, hitting the poor beasts.
A lthough, the green baby dino in the egg was sealed in a hole,
U ntil the little dinosaur was dug up by a curious mole.
R ealising he was in a modern era,
S trange machines zooming by at great speed, moving nearer and nearer.

D inosaurs weren't meant for this time period,
O nly one way for the baby to fit in -
M aybe to make a friend.
I ncredibly, his luck was great, when someone put him in a shop.
N o one came, but when he nearly lost his spark of hope,
A little girl said, "This one, please."
T he girl's name was Isabelle, and she named him Horny.
E very day, he was loved, and he was never alone again.

Isabelle Fennelly (11)
Bungay High School, Bungay

The Mega Onion

One day I was cooking,
While around I was looking,
I picked up a knife,
It was as sharp as a scythe.

And then an onion I picked up,
I placed him down in a cup.
Then the onion arose in a specific pose,
Then he said, "Hey,"
Like a horse going neigh.

But then the onion said:
There is no brain in your head.
Sadly that is kinda true,
"Oh, and something else, you stink of poo."

Then I started to cry,
"Oh just shut up, you're as daft as a fly,"
I started to shout for my mummy,
As the butterflies flew in my tummy.

Then she came,
Oh how much I was in pain.
"He hurt my feelings,"
"Who?"
"Him,"
"He's an onion."

Then the onion arose,
In a specific pose,
Then he said "Hey,"
Like a horse going neigh.

Then my mummy fainted,
Like something scary being painted,
But then my tummy rumbled,
That made my house rock and tumble.

I threw him in the oven,
And said, "You're as mean as a coven."
"I'm just a poor onion,
Please don't burn my bunion."

I started to cook him alive,
While I danced the jive,
Suddenly the oven stopped
As his skin sizzled and popped.

I scoffed him down,
Through my stomach's town.
Now he's a big, big, big, big, big, big, big, big, big lump of stinky poo,
And guess what - now you know how to deal with nasty onions too!

Oliver Hall (12)
Bungay High School, Bungay

Whispers Of Radiant Realities

In the quiet of the night, under twinkling stars,
Lies the beautiful truth hidden from afar.
A truth so pure, so gentle and bright,
A truth that fills our hearts with delight.

It whispers in the rustling leaves,
And dances in the morning breeze.
It paints the world in vibrant hues,
And breathes life into the dullest blues.

The beautiful truth is all around,
In the laughter of a child, in the music's sound.
It speaks of the gentle wave that kisses the shore,
And in the love that we all adore.

It blooms in the mundane, in the mundane's embrace,
In a hand that holds steady, a warm, tender face...
It's alive with passion, with love and grace,
And it's always wear a smile on our face.

So let this truth guide your way,
And fill your heart with joy each day.
For in its embrace, you'll find peace and light,
And bask in the beauty of the beautiful truth's might.

So let us behold it, this beautiful truth,
Embrace its soft edges, reclaim our lost youth.

For in every heartbeat, in love's gentle plea,
Lies a truth that is boundless forever in we...

Angelyn Johny (12)
Bungay High School, Bungay

Panic Attack

The world no longer matters.
As people sit there doing nothing,
I panic.
I go frantic.
I want to rip out my hair,
Bang my head on my chair,
I want to go mad.
But I can't.
And I won't
Panic.
But I can't force it back,
And I want to calm down,
I want to cry,
Do anything just to stop,
Wondering why,
Oh, why can't I just die,
Why can't this end?
And then as quickly as it came,
It goes,
So I don't panic.

Mia Macfarlane (13)
Bungay High School, Bungay

Clocks

Tick-tock, tick-tock goes the hands of the clock.
Clomp, clomp, clomp go the feet down the hallway.
Click, click, click, click go the gears in the clock,
Suddenly, silence.
Gong, gong, gong goes the clock to strike midday.

Ryan Page (11)
Bungay High School, Bungay

Dog, Doll And A Man

I am a doll,
I sit pretty on a throne of praise
I bow after a dazzling display
I don't speak, only mouth the words
I'm made to say,
And a new expression is engraved on my face
When I slip, I shatter,
When I fall, I am destroyed
In his hands, I falter,
In his hands, I grow frail,
But in that time of trouble
You took me in your warm embrace
And showed me a kind face
But who's to say it was all a play
My memories are nothing but a daze

I miss my doll
A doll with a silly dance
How will that help me advance
I realise I need not a toy but a man's best friend
But now friend and foe are blurred in your midst,
You are no ordinary pet.
You would rather feast on flesh than play fetch
You seem more of a beast at best,
So different from the rest,
However, my own moral slate is not clean or delicate,
The malice that lies in me

Is one not even you can replicate,
But I need you by my side.
That is where man's best friend resides,
But now I have gathered an army of hounds
Who will break and shatter every straining bounds.
Who will submit to the gamble of my schemes
Who sees you as no more than feeble prey,
And have you trembling in your place,
Oh... But to see you die for my sake,
No, there is no time for regret, sorrow or mistakes,
I can only look towards tomorrow's sun,
Yesterday is already miles behind me,
What's done is done,
I could see beyond the clouds,
And I can only think out loud,
I'm already so many metres high,
I can feel my feet lifting off the ground,
And shooting for the sky.

Tear me from my lead,
And rip out my eye,
Saw off my arm,
But I am still your dog,
And you are my doll,
I want to see you whole again,
At least one more time,
But with just one eye,
Even half of your beauty is enough for me,

I am malicious, you are misshapen,
A forgotten masterpiece,
But you still look so brilliant in my memory,
Your moves were full of passion and pride,
But your once bustling audience has now died,
But wilting in the once vacant seat,
A dog and that is me.

Blossom Uzoigwe (15)
Macmillan Academy, Middlesbrough

The Olive Tree

The olive trees are dying.
The familiar scent of laughter and joy was nowhere to be found.
All to be seen were the bombings and screams of terror.
When the voices of young children were no longer heard in the violent lands.
Where once the olive trees, who were content with blissful love were now dying in the perils of the land.
The young girl all alone tucked in a corner,
Lay saddened by her martyred family,
While hoping every day all the violence would end,
And hoped for nothing but peace and unity for her country.
But it's been seventy-six years of fighting non-stop.
All peace was soon consumed by trauma and slowly took over the hearts of the citizens.
To what was once a home filled with memories and adventures,
Was now replaced by the haunting screams of silence.
The olive trees are dying,
Yet the world fails to see,
Can't they smell the burning of your agony?

Fridaus Juma (13)
Macmillan Academy, Middlesbrough

A Long Journey In My Life

Life's journey began with twists and turns.
At eight, a loss, a heart that yearns.
My dad's departure, a heavy blow,
A young heart learning to cope and grow.

My brother in foster, a separate path,
Yet my grandparents' love is like a warm, gentle bath.
Nana and Grandad, their arms so wide,
Gave me a place to lay beside.

My mum moved away, left an arrow in my heart.
Which slowly made us drift apart.
Christian teachings, a guiding light
Through the darkest days and endless ongoing nights.

Football became my saving grace
On the field, I then found my place.
Each goal a victory, a story told
In every match, my spirit was bold.

Through trials faced and battles won
My journey has just begun.
In life's grand game, I play my part
With strength and courage and a loving heart.

Alexis Jaques (12)
Macmillan Academy, Middlesbrough

One Chance

In a world where whispers chase the sun,
Dreams dance lightly, one by one,
Through fields of laughter, colours blend,
Every moment is magic, around each bend.

With a heart full of stories, waiting to unfold,
Adventures lie hidden, yet to be told,
From the stars above to the ocean's sway,
Life's a canvas, I'll paint it my way.

Catch the breeze, let it sway your thoughts,
Find joy in the little things life forgot,
Splash in puddles, run wild and free,
Embrace all the wonders of what can be.

Turn my gaze toward the setting sun,
Cherish each heartbeat, this life is a fun run,
So I'll take a step forward, letting my spirit ignite,
In the glow of tomorrow, everything feels right.

Aisha Hussain (12)
Macmillan Academy, Middlesbrough

The Lies Of A Good Friend

In the veil of dreams,
A friend's breath, a serpent coil,
Truths torn at the seams.

Beneath moonlit skies,
Lies dance in silken whispers,
Veiled conflict implied.

Once shared laughter gleamed,
Now shadows stretch, haunting tales,
Anger's bitter seam.

In gardens of trust,
Thorns grow where roses had bloomed,
Fingers stained with dust.

Nightmares unfurl deep,
Fragrant mists that shroud the past,
Secrets buried steep.

Betrayed by the light,
Hope flickers like a candle,
A heart turned to night.

Footsteps echo wide,
Recover from this sorrow,
Yet fight for the pride.

Gothic tales unfold,
In betrayal's dark embrace,
Lost dreams turn to gold.

Faith Williams (12)
Macmillan Academy, Middlesbrough

Paradise

They return to the trench after a long hard day of work,
After another endless endeavour,
And home is tainted by glorious battle scars,
Where fear unceasingly drowns them.

Soldiers never liberate from the dreaded commitment.

They serve for the powerful clan they're obliged to,
Bequeathing years of brutal sacrifice.
For whose benefit?
They're put to work in never-ending horrors,
Slashed by treacherous thorns.

We live in an uneven Paradise.

Another man receives dazzling coins for his commendation,
For every shackle that he's bound by,
Trapped in the trench that he escaped from.

Imogen Stockton (14)
Macmillan Academy, Middlesbrough

The Owl

How the owl into the womb of heaven soars,
Its wings glistening in the light of the moon,
It's shriek sounding out over the empty moors.

At peace and carefree in the night skies of June,
Not a care in the world, just simple and free,
Hidden by cover during the height of the moon.

Over the roofs of forests and shining sea,
Under skies of stars and over swathes of green,
Watching from rooftops and the branch of a tree.

The owl is free and intelligent and keen,
The owl is innocent and beautiful and clean.

Lorelei Myers (13)
Macmillan Academy, Middlesbrough

Much To Do

Writing, singing, much to do.
Dogs go woof and cows go moo.
Much to do, there and here.
Play sports, or go to the pier.

Many precious moments people waste.
Many fears, people conquered and faced.
Go outside, have a nice time.
Like me, making this poem rhyme.

With so much to do, why waste it doing nothing?
How much happiness could that bring?
Never waste the opportunities life gives you.
But doing everything is hard, that is true.

Skye Mockett (12)
Macmillan Academy, Middlesbrough

If Only

Her bright and warm smile
You can see from hundreds of miles
Her radiant and fair skin
As colourful and vibrant as a fish's fin
The happy and lively girl I once knew
The flower blooming in the midst of darkness
The warm and pleasant girl that could lighten up your day...
Is now... gone
The air now stuffy and suffocating
As she slowly disappears
If only I'd known
If only I could go back and change the past
If only
If only...

Deborah Oshode (12)
Macmillan Academy, Middlesbrough

Rubescent Lies

I am of no fixed abode,
All of this numbing ecstasy you've bestowed upon me,
Why?
Why have your eyes landed upon me?
To what degree do you see me as equal?
I just know deep down inside that you'll be lethal.
But it's comfortable, really,
You provide me solace.
But what is solace if I've never felt contrary to it?
Your red, recurrent touch,
With your smoke coming up to the sky,
Why did I never see through your rubescent lies?

Martha Towers (14)
Macmillan Academy, Middlesbrough

School

I wake up early,
Just to panic,
Trying to look happy,
My mind problematic.

I stare at the clock,
My mind overthinking,
Thoughts locked,
Staring as the clock goes tick-tock.

I come out of my mind,
As the bell rings,
My teeth grind,
My thoughts swing.

I feel exhausted,
But I am not even done,
I have 1826 days left,
And haven't even finished day one.

Sian Large (12)
Macmillan Academy, Middlesbrough

Trust No One

T he echo of his voice
R uns through my mind
U sing his powers
S o carelessly
T hey, him, will not stop

N ever will I speak truth
O nly when he lies dead

O nly then will I trust again
N o one will see the truth my
E verlasting fear.

Esther Golden (12)
Macmillan Academy, Middlesbrough

School

School is a place for education
And I will not try to use exaggeration
In school, you can learn English, maths and science
Or, if you want, you can form an alliance
There are so many things that you can do
When you see the school doors and step right through.

Tyler Saunders (12)
Macmillan Academy, Middlesbrough

The Real Me

Crying
Hiding
Trying
Lying
When I was young
I'd cry for attention
Now that I'm all grown up
I hide
Everything
Even the real me
She's locked in a room
Further than she should be
I put on a fake me
A fake personality
Even in my home
The real me is sporty
Loves art
Adores science and likes geography
But me
The fake me
Thinks school is useless
And learning is pointless
And it's slowly
Starting
To dye the real me
I hang out with my so-called friends

Even though we have a massive group and drama every week
It's never interesting, they're all the same
And I feel lonely
Knowing
That they would hate me for me
When can I show the real me?
When will I show the real me?
When can I be set free?
My routine of hiding, crying, trying, and lying is starting to affect me
My room slowly shrinks as I'm being forgotten
I miss the feeling of being loved for me
But at this point
It's just a lost cause and a waste of hope
The real me.

Tolu Opesanwo (13)
Magna Academy, Canford Heath

I Am Me

I am me,
Me I may be.
But here I am writing for what I saw,
And what I see.

Through tough times,
And watching mimes,
I am me.

From being here,
To going there,
I am me.

Life is a horror,
But it can be a fantasy,
For the life of me,
Is good and bad.

Part one or one part,
Of the life of me,
Through hard times,
And big climbs,
I am me.

Cheering on my favourite team,
To becoming a team,
I am me.

I am Steve,
I can believe,
It is possible,
To have a good life,
But it won't change,
That I am me.

I am who I'm meant to be,
And as I say again and again,
That I am me.

Be who you want to be,
Do what you want to do,
But in the end,
You are you,
And I am me.

Life is us,
And we are life.
I believe life will be amazing,
And life will change,
But in the end,
You are you,
And I am me.

Don't change yourself because of or for others.
Just be you.

Milo Buck (13)
Magna Academy, Canford Heath

The Beautiful Truth Of Holt United Football

We've done it!
We have won the League
We have been promoted to Division One
Now we have a different task, it's a big ask
Back-to-back titles, is it possible?
Holt United League Cup runners-up
County Cup semi-finalists
Division Two winners

You will find the truth of football out on the pitch
There it lies
All the answers can arise
The beautiful truth lies on the football pitch
But sometimes the truth leaves you in a ditch
And then everything is left there
Not always with the pitch but with the scoreboard
This is the betrayal of the truth in football

The beautiful truth is what gives us a path
To achieve and succeed
The question is can we beat the champs?
Can we steal the crown and see others bow?
The beautiful truth gives us that aspiration to achieve

The beautiful truth may not be winning but having the blessing to play the beautiful game of football
The beautiful truth of football.

Noah Clinton (13)
Magna Academy, Canford Heath

Black Prejudice

B eing black shows lots of things: bad things, good things, all of the above.
L ots of people are all different in the end, they all push and shove.
A nd many others make racial slurs, comments etc etc.
C ountless others would join in and behave in such a way.
K nots and ties, screws and bolts, snap, crackle, pop!

P eople say, when it's done, it's done.
R eady to learn, that's heavily not true.
E ven though it still lingers in my brain.
J ust know what I say is all okay. Learn from mistakes.
U nder my black skin are bones, organs and everything else.
D iscouraged by the truth to be told.
I n the night, the dark shows a hint of bold.
C ome with me, listen up good. You're perfect. Just misunderstood.
E nter the world as it shows, back, white, mixed. All good. This is black prejudice.

Ty'ron Bello (13)
Magna Academy, Canford Heath

The Wright Brother's Success

1904, a great year for sure,
People had made boats,
But the Wright brothers wanted more,
As they tried, the first brother confessed,
"My pride and work has come to rest,"
The second brother cried,
This made him try harder,
Until one day, he made something impossible.
An aircraft! A plane! Nothing went to shame!
The first brother came and said, "You little brain!"
And then, the day arrived,
The day to take flight,
And it worked, it really worked,
Today, 2024, there have been so many flights,
Thanks to the Wrights,
And many other achievements,
21st January, 1974,
Arrived a plane called Concorde,
Goes at Mach 2,
Everyone thought it was impossible too!
25th October, 2007,
A double-decker plane comes,
After 1987, over seven million flights every year,
This is all possible, thanks to the Wrights.

Max Simpson (12)
Magna Academy, Canford Heath

Unique

You are you
You know who to be
You know you're a person
So go and be free
You have to stand tall
Just like a tree
Don't just let go and flee
I listen to my song going on repeat
You can relax
Here, take a seat
We are people, we are prior
We can run and spread like a wildfire
You are unique
That's really new
You will have to be there
You know what to do
You aren't old
You're not an antique
And for that reason
You are unique
Your life runs
It's basically a loop
You are different
Better than a group
I don't know what to say
But you are brighter

Than the sun's ray
You are not different
You're in the picture
Do your best and you'll win the fixture
We can achieve greatness together in three
You are you
That's who you'll be.

Lucas Cornachini Paiva
Magna Academy, Canford Heath

Handball

When I play handball,
I have fun.
I play for England.
In handball,
it is like a ball of power, in my hands.

When I get the ball,
I like to pass or dribble around opponents.
In handball, you only have three steps.
If you take more without dribbling,
It goes to the other team.
But you can do something called a dribble.

A dribble is where you bounce the ball,
But if you bounce it and then hold it,
then dribble again,
It goes to the other team.
This is called a double dribble.

If you dribble, you can't pick it back up
You have to do something,
Like a shot or a pass.
When you have the ball,
You only have three seconds without a dribble,
If you hold it for longer than three seconds
The other team gets the ball.

Handball is fun.
Handball makes me happy.
Harry Lawrence (12)
Magna Academy, Canford Heath

Two Sides Or More

Music,
A simple thing,
Yet complex,
Colourful,
Yet seen in black and white,
Opera,
Yet rock and roll,
Makes you dance,
Huge part of me before,
And will be after,
Dance,
Fun,
Yet competitive,
Self-confident,
Yet, jealous,
Emotional,
Yet funky,
Boxing,
You get hit,
But also the hitter,
You are trained,
But your mind is on your own trainer,
You defend,
But defeated,
Everything has two sides,
People have more,

Strong side,
Happy side,
Sad side,
The side you never want to see,
The ones already long gone,
Yet seem so close,
Always remember,
You are worth it all,
Even at the peak of awful,
You are worth walking this Earth,
The world would miss your footprints,
Use your worth.

Quinn Rickard-Muller (13)
Magna Academy, Canford Heath

It's Not Fair

It's not fair that young girls have to fight to play,
But boys don't have that struggle,
"Name five players," I hate that.

It's not fair that they think,
That women's football is not real football,
But we all grew up idolising the same players,
So why is it not just football?

"She just got lucky,"
"She'll never make it,"
Simple words they all say,
But they will never understand how much it hurts to hear,
When everyone believes in their dreams.

It's not fair, we girls want it to be an equal environment,
But how long do we have to fight,
For them to realise that girls just want to be taken seriously in the sports industry?
Why can't it just be fair?

Mirela Manea (14)
Magna Academy, Canford Heath

School Rules

Do not shout, do not laugh,
Please be quiet, do not be daft.
Do not whine, do not cheat,
Hey, look at me when I speak.

Be sensible, stay alert,
You must fit in, do not get hurt.
Being responsible is the biggest thing,
But when Miss talks, my ears ring!

Do not forget, do not ignore,
Soon you'll hear me start to snore.
Do not be silly, keep your head up!
Gum in your hair? You don't have much luck.

Screaming, staring you start 'not caring',
The feeble attempts on the story they're telling.
Listen, shut up, no, why not?
These words on repeat, your brain starts to rot.

My mind turns to mush, mindless animatronics,
I might not be rich, but at least I know my phonics.

Danni Popa (13)
Magna Academy, Canford Heath

Wildfires Of The Present

Born as a dim flame,
But not as hot as a sun,
I won't stay the same,
Not even a cheetah can run.

I am now spreading,
Consuming everything in sight,
They don't think I'm a bedding
All creatures will be given a monstrous fright.

Rabbits and rejected pets are running for their lives,
Some are trapped and have to accept fate,
Like a bee flies away from a hive,
They'll do nothing as it's too late.

People think I'm a liar,
Unlike trees, I can bend
But my pants are on fire,
It's now the end.

I woke up, but it was just a dream,
Wait... why am I blasting a beam?
Oh no! My hands aren't clean,
But don't worry, they can't be seen.

Anabelle Harris (12)
Magna Academy, Canford Heath

The Deep Blue

Sometimes I wonder if I'm real,
Or if everything's just a dream where no one can heal,
Now I'm at a dock, leaning into the blue,
Further and further with no clue.

There I am sinking into the void,
No one can convince me I'm real with a coin,
Down, down, down, there's no going back,
My family isn't real, a dog or a cat,

The void is endless, deeper and deeper,
I'm going further, creepier and creepier,
Maybe this is how they hide the void,
Empty and dark with no noise.

Wait, what's that? Nothing happened,
Sat at the dock, with a lantern,
Sometimes I wonder if I'm real,
Or the void is there waiting to heal...

Zara Hausawi (12)
Magna Academy, Canford Heath

Behind Closed Doors

I'm just a kid
Behind closed doors
Cooking, cleaning
Taking care of my brother
All by myself.
My hands are dry
Pale from bleach.

I'm just a kid
Behind closed doors
Plaster a smile
Be the joker
Don't let the mask slip
Otherwise, they'll see.

The feeling of emptiness
Inside me is unmatched.
The pressure of the world
On my shoulders.

"Detention," he says
I'm too loud.
"Not good enough," she says,
As my eyes grow heavy.
No one knows.
No one knows how it really feels.

But I'm just a kid
Behind closed doors
Plaster a smile
Be the joker.
Keep going.

Jack Parsons (12)
Magna Academy, Canford Heath

'Beautiful' Truths

I feel alone but people surround me,
I act like a person I'm not supposed to be,
Dark alleys, dark corners, dark thoughts,
No one asked why I quit my favourite sport,
The night treats me better than 'friends',
I don't know if I'll ever be on the mend,
They'll ask if I'm okay,
What do they care anyway?
I don't know what's worse,
So many terrible things in this universe,
They said beauty is natural, really,
Did they mean it? Barely,
Lonely again? They can't know,
They don't care when I am low,
I don't know how much more I can bear,
They talk to me as if it was a dare,
All this time now, I've started to prepare.

Rubie Burt (13)
Magna Academy, Canford Heath

Late Night Halloween

H ouses stocked with sweets
A frightening sound from the woods
L ate nights, the sky looks like a void
L onely roads stretch and bend
O ne bowl filled with sweets
W eird, ridiculous costumes everywhere
E very house flickering with orange and purple lights
E ven adults have sweets
N o one is sad

C hill air blows into my face
O range pumpkins on every porch
S trange laughs come from all around
T all trees tower over me in the darkness
U p the roads, more houses lay
M y hands go cold and numb
E ating everything in my sweet bowl
S ounds echo in the air.

Cohen Rutt (12)
Magna Academy, Canford Heath

Football Is Life, Football Is Everything

Two teams, one ball,
Ninety minutes to decide it all,
Football is life, football is everything,
Ninety minutes of hearts racing,
Ninety minutes of ball chasing,
This is more than just an ordinary sport,
It has emotions of all sorts,
I gaze across the pitch,
At the perfectly cut grass,
Will I score?
Will I make that pass?
What other sports make the whole world stop and stare?
What other sport can have the smallest team's city care?
From friends to enemies,
From enemies to friends,
New careers begin,
But some end,
Some call it football,
Some call it soccer,
Some play for anger,
Some play for healing,
Two names, one same feeling.

Zac Wilson (13)
Magna Academy, Canford Heath

Stray Kids

Chris, Felix, Lee Know
The names keep flowing through my mind like the ocean
Movements of a peacock, voices of angels, raps as quick as light
Eat healthy, don't hurt yourself
More and more promises to keep but get broken
The first, Chris, born to be an idol
The second, Lee Know, heart of gold set on someone
The third, Hyunjin, moves as swift as a bird
The fourth, Changbin, a voice made like the flash
The fifth, Han, his heart set on another of gold
The sixth, Felix, his voice makes you warm
The seventh, Seungmin, a devil with an angel's voice
Finally, I.N, young and able, hardworking and silly
Eight together make one,
This is Stray Kids.

Renesmee Bennett (13)
Magna Academy, Canford Heath

My Nightmare

Do you remember the night?
The night my little sister screamed
Like a fox
Howling in the night
The night smoke
Engulfed my lungs
My heart vibrated
My ribcage
My eyes burned
Stung
Smoke cascaded in my room
Swirling
Twirling
It sped at lightning speed
Swallowing
Everything
Whole
It was like a cheetah running
It banged at my door
Calling it to let me in
No escape
No escape
Smash!
I busted my window open
People's feet clattered against
The cold metal staircase

It burst open my door
Ready for a midnight feast
The night that haunts me still.
Do you remember the night?

Zoe Fox (12)
Magna Academy, Canford Heath

Dungeon Of Dreams

I had a dream,
A dream trapped in my head,
I didn't know what it could mean,
I thought of it while I lay in bed,
However, it was locked in the dungeon of dreams,
Impossible to unlock, it seemed.

I had a dream,
A dream trapped in my head,
I soared through the sky, it seemed,
I thought of it while I lay in bed,
However, it was locked in the dungeon of dreams,
The key thrown away, it seemed.

I had a dream,
A dream trapped in my head,
I climbed into a plane, it seemed,
I thought of it while I lay in bed,
This time, there was no lock at the dungeon of dreams,
I grabbed my dream, motivated to accomplish it, it seemed.

Ryan Earl (13)
Magna Academy, Canford Heath

Love As A Drug

Love is a drug,
And I am its willing slave,
Caught in the haze of its pull,
Riding highs I can't explain,

Each breath is laced with you,
Each thought a dose too sweet,
My heart, an addict craving more,
Of the fire you make me feel,

I lose myself in the rush,
The chaos of your touch,
Chasing the thrill of your voice,
Your smile, the hit I can't give up,

But love is a poison too,
A needle that sinks too deep,
Its bite can tear me open,
Leave me cold and weak,

Still, I drink you in,
Knowing the cost,
Because of the price of withdrawal,
Is a price I won't bear, even if I'm lost.

Nade Hawkins (13)
Magna Academy, Canford Heath

My Halloween Nightmares

My nightmares come to life
At night when darkness creeps into my mind
All houses, streets, and corners were decorated
Pumpkins, skeletons and spiders
All children dressed up
Their costumes of ghosts
Zombies, witches, and the devil
Squeals and screams echo
My heart flutters
A zombie with a shadow for a face
The one who haunts my dreams
Suddenly costumes transformed
To terrifying creatures
Pumpkins transformed into monsters
With red, wild eyes
Blood rain
I blink away the blurry film
Covering my eyes
As I awake to the sight of ruins
Walls smashed
Shadows looming
I live inside my nightmares.

Nataliia Sokol (12)
Magna Academy, Canford Heath

A Special Moment

I was sat on the beach, calm and chilled
The sea splattering onto the soft, grainy sand and then to my feet

The smile of my parents
Happy that we had finally left our always-raining country
Their sparkling eyes being shone on by the sun

I walked into the cold, blue sea
My heart calm as ever
The temperature of the sea made me shiver
I splashed the water with my hands to cool me down

As I looked around, seeing the scenery around me
The ruined castle as old as my great grandparents' parents
The tall buildings where people have lived for lifetimes on end
But also the loud music coming from the streets.

Ben Sims (13)
Magna Academy, Canford Heath

Fighting For Football

Girls all over the world,
One sport,
One passion,
Football.

Fighting for football,
Something we have to do,
Sexist views widespreading,
Young girls unknowing how to fight it.

"Girls can't play football."
The common phrase, too common,
Words which seem normal,
Words which cut so deep.

Women's football,
A normal phrase,
Right?
However when men play, it's just football.

Why's it so funny when I try my best,
Meanwhile when they do it,
They're hardworking,
But I'll never make it, right?

Will we have to fight forever?

Sophia Epton (13)
Magna Academy, Canford Heath

Van Gogh's Sweet Insanity

How can someone else see everything when I see nothing?
Everyone can see the truth but not me
Am I really that bad, that crazy?
Confined to a tiny 'chambre'
No longer in my 'bedroom in Arles'

A constant image of Mr Gauguin, such an insulter
I can't stand his voice, so I made it disappear
Silence, blood spewing all on the floor
It's the same sweet crimson red from my beloved towel
Paul's image still remains but his voice is quieter

Finally, the bit of recognition I deserve
Only too late for me to see
I still hear the loud shot
Louder than Paul Gauguin's voice ever was.

Emma Caseley (14)
Magna Academy, Canford Heath

Why Bully?

Too many people judged on the way they look
Never judge a book by its cover
Bullying could lead to mental health issues or worse
It's like theft
Taking someone's soul
Sometimes it's too hard to get them back to whole!

Bullying is a mouse vs tiger
Smaller vs bigger
It's like a piece of paper
You crumble it over and over
Once you say sorry, the paper opens
But still there is a worry
The paper is still damaged
This is like bullying
They are still hurting...

They might continue on their own life
But they will still remember
The worst time of their life...

Rodin Turan (13)
Magna Academy, Canford Heath

Southampton Football Club

Southampton is my favourite team,
Although they are not that good, it would seem.
Signing Ramsdale was the best choice known to man,
Even though I'm the only fan.

Back down to the Championship we'll go,
In all honesty, I preferred it down there though.
We have not won a game this whole season for all.
The team are Cinderella, they run away from the ball.

We'll win the Premier League, so you'll see,
Just don't be Jack Stephens and swear at the referee.
The only good thing Southampton fans can say,
Is that Shane Long has scored the fastest Premier League goal to this day.

Oliver Malone (14)
Magna Academy, Canford Heath

The Beautiful Truth

Football is the beautiful truth, my truth.
Football is the greatest lesson, a metaphor for life.
Nothing's forever, ninety minutes, time's limited, enjoy it.
Everything can change in seconds
Big matches, big events, some adrenaline.
Football, my escape, alternate reality.
Box nets, astro pitches, my beautiful truth
The biggest supporter is always there
Family and friends may leave, football's forever
Football is my best decision
Football gave me the best friends I will ever have
Football has given me so many amazing opportunities
Football is the beautiful truth, my truth.

Amelia Conroy (13)
Magna Academy, Canford Heath

A Christmas Cave

I was tumbling in the snow,
I rolled like an unknown mole,
I stumbled upon a crazy cave
With low snow over its face.
Its dark appearance made my fate.
My heart pounding like a drum
In an open stage,
I walked in with courage.
Shock shot my heart.
It was loaded with golden presents.
My eyes thought it was a dream.
There were elves with spiky tips for shoes,
One saw me and
Gave a devastating glare.
They started to stumble over to me
And greeted me nicely,
But I declined and ran away,
And that secret is
Still with me today.

Leo Waddington (12)
Magna Academy, Canford Heath

The Day Of The Horse Race

We were off like the wind.
In my head I sang
I could feel the rhythm of the horse on the race course
It was the day of the race
People thought it was a disgrace
My heart thumped out of my chest
This was going to be the best
It was the final stretch
My horse went faster and faster
It knew I was its master
The line was ahead
I wished I was in bed
We galloped faster than ever
I didn't care about the weather
We had finished the race!
And I had a wonderful pace
What a miracle!
Me and my horse won.

Jessica Miller (12)
Magna Academy, Canford Heath

Two Lovers

The two lovers
Different people that wish they were the same
In school, don't talk, they're secret lovers
One day they go to Asda,
They buy a parrot because it is on sale
They name it Bob
One day it dies from something thick and long
They feel bad for Bob
One day they go into the forest and they get lost
After two months they both secretly like each other
But don't tell each other
After another one month they find their way out
And tell each other that they like each other
And live happily ever after.

Lewis Ashdown (13)
Magna Academy, Canford Heath

What Have We Done?!

So much carbon in the air,
I don't know why,
But it just isn't fair!

Many cars powered by petrol,
Maybe diesel too,
But now the trees are dying,
And soon we will be too!

All of these palm oil plants,
Are spreading like fleas,
Destroying the rainforests,
Like a terrible disease.

But we can all help,
And do some good soon,
Electric-powered cars,
Or populating the moon!

So much carbon in the air,
We just need to help ourselves,
To get somewhere!

Oliver Stevenson (13)
Magna Academy, Canford Heath

My Phone

My phone,
my phone is like a deathtrap,
but there's no escape,
no freedom,
Oh look, a new trend,
worse than the last,
Donald Trump with drinking bleach,
And P Diddy taking over my screen.

The future,
my phone superglued to my hand,
no escape,
big screen everywhere,
the brain rot is real,
kids' mental health going further through the roof.
All the magazines,
why don't I look like them?
My phone is like a deathtrap,
no freedom and no escape, we're stuck.

Daisy Hall (13)
Magna Academy, Canford Heath

Deep Sleep

Wouldn't it be nice to sleep forever
To relax our tired souls
The beauty is the stance that calms us
Like an empty field overlooking the sea
Je to krasna vec (it's a beautiful thing)
That we can escape to
Where our mind can rest and feel safe
Wouldn't it be easier if we slept forever
Not bothered by war, fakes, or the world's issues
But in the end, being a nocturnal is not a career
The relaxation of our minds is not eternal
And slowly the comfort is taken away.

Jakub Labik (13)
Magna Academy, Canford Heath

11,000 Rpm

There's a point, 11000 rpm, where everything fades.

There's a point,
Where your exhaust screams,
So you don't have to.

There's a point,
Your brakes take the pressure,
That you once carried.

There's a point,
Your steering wheel changes direction,
The one that could make or break you.

There's a point,
Your seat holds someone,
The person you dreamt of being.

That was the point at 11,000 rpm, where it all faded.

Oscar Stockley-King (13)
Magna Academy, Canford Heath

My Gruesome Feelings

I'm not a clone,
I'm not what you say I am,
I'm just me;
Same old me.
Insecure about everything,
Locked in my room all day, every day,
Trapped in a cage of thoughts.
This endless loop of hiding, crying and fake smiles,
When will it all end?
When will I be able to think of myself as a normal human?
I have a heart, a brain and feelings,
I try my best to be perfect enough for them to like me;
It's never enough.
I'm done.
I'm always alone.

Libbie Gurd (12)
Magna Academy, Canford Heath

It's Okay

Fine, I'll admit it.
The world isn't really my biggest fan at the moment.
Not everything about me is in order,
And I'm not really sure where I may be in five years time.
All these questions unravel out of my mind,
And yet, all the questions are still left unanswered.
But it doesn't really matter anymore,
Because it's okay to be not okay.
Day by day,
Year by year.
It will all be okay,
As you slowly find your way to peace.

Maya-Louise Rammell (13)
Magna Academy, Canford Heath

Fake It Till You Make It

M y mind is against me
E veryone thinks I'm okay
N obody knows
T eachers try to help me
A tear drops on my book
L essons are draining

H appy faces, nobody knows
E veryone thinks I'm happy, nobody knows
A nother tear drops, nobody knows
L augh, perhaps it wasn't that deep
T ell someone you're okay, nobody knows
H appy face, nobody knows.

Karabo Baitshoki (13)
Magna Academy, Canford Heath

Pressure

The doors shoot open
I walk out of the boat
I grab the keycard on the desk
Water splashes at me
I open a door
I loot the drawers scattered around the room
The lights flickered
Leaving me shaken
A quick sound of screeching enters my ear
I sprint into the water
Parasites covering me
I grab my flashbang and chuck it
The screeching gets louder
I enter a tunnel
I end up on the beach
I'm never going there again.

Max Richardson (12)
Magna Academy, Canford Heath

The Truth Of Football

True or false?
They say that beauty is football,
You will find your truth in time,
But is time real?

One day, I found beauty.
When I was a little kid.
My truth lives on yourself,
Football is time, but is time real?

You will find the truth out on the pitch.
Is football the beauty of truth?
Football is hard, so is it beauty?
But you don't see beauty on the pitch.
So, is beauty football?

Mason Urbanski (13)
Magna Academy, Canford Heath

Canvas

E motions are like a canvas, splattering all around.
M omentum to get the courage to speak out for help.
O nly listen to good, be like a canvas and have no limitations.
T rust, you need to find someone to trust.
I ce dripping into the bucket, ready to spill like a waterfall.
O ral trust, speak as if you are a waterfall, speak and let it flow.
N oise, make noise to drown out the bad.
S ad, but don't be bad.

Noah-Kythe Hemnebelle (13)
Magna Academy, Canford Heath

The Lucky One

"I'm the lucky one," I cheered,
Free upgrade to first class,
Reclining seats, extra leg room,
How lucky can one be?

The captain's panicked voice came on the radio,
Oxygen masks dropped as we fell in altitude.
Seatbelt sign came on and alarms were wailing.
I blacked out.

Plane wing in a tree,
Luggage squished my feet,
Everyone dead but me,
The lucky one.

Callum Bourton (12)
Magna Academy, Canford Heath

The Loop

I check I turned my straighteners off,
Then check it twice, maybe three times,
Just to feel nice,
The lights?
They're off, but I must make sure,
Flick them once more, then I'm sure.

Lines must be straight, everything balanced,
Hands are washed, but not qiute yet,
A couple more scrubs.

My brain is like a loop,
Round and round,
Order's the way to calm it down.

Shyanne Taylor (13)
Magna Academy, Canford Heath

Fortnite

The station that I pulled up at was Reckless Railways.
The front of the train went down like a frown.
The Channel of people slowly died.
The silver bullets rained down.
A car drifted around the corner,
For the glory of a Victory Royale.

Victory Royale won,
Teleporting back to lobby,
Looking at the Item Shop,
Want a skin,
Bought a skin.
V-bucks lost.
Time for another win.

Robert Heed (13)
Magna Academy, Canford Heath

Broken Bridge

The beautiful truth is,
War is violent.
A broken bridge?
Broken hearts.
A broken bridge?
Broken shelter.
May I ask why we do this?
For land and power, we all say,
But are you just doing it for money's sake?
A broken bridge?
Broken bombshells.
A broken bridge?
Broken relationship,
So may I ask once again,
Why do we do this?
For money's sake.

Humaid Hussain (12)
Magna Academy, Canford Heath

Anger

A pencil can be sharp or blunt
But sometimes they can break
Just like your thoughts and mind
But you have to keep it in
But no matter how hard you try it will come out
You will pop and burst and explode in anger
And you just can't help it
So don't focus on it
Be happy, calm and nice
Don't turn down once-in-a-lifetime opportunities
All because you're angry.

Baylee Pittam (12)
Magna Academy, Canford Heath

The Best Halloween Ever!

On the night of Halloween,
Which was the best night of all,
Not a creature to be seen,
Not a creature to crawl,
It's a night that makes people happy.

It's not that peaceful, but makes me feel at peace,
It's about going to a house, asking for sweets,
But all that's to say is, trick or treat,
But if you like the lady or man you might say they're sweet.

Miyah Elizabeth-Skye Mangan (13)
Magna Academy, Canford Heath

My Dog Ted

I have a crazy dog,
His name is Teddy and he's very friendly.
Ted's always excited and loves to have visitors,
He loves to go on walks
But will bark at anything or anyone
Who goes past as he wants to say hello.
Ted mostly seems happy and joyful,
But sometimes he can be down and sad
But never bad.
He likes to sleep, eat, and play,
But most of all he loves me.

Millie Brown (13)
Magna Academy, Canford Heath

Christmas Joy

One very joyful morning,
With lots of Christmas joy and cheer,
The family opened all the presents,
Under the tall, colourful tree.
Then they went outside to watch the snow fall,
Making hot chocolate that was the best taste of all,
Going sleighing and sitting by the fire.
Christmas is the best season,
I wish it would never end,
Can't wait for it to come once again.

Briley Hayward (12)
Magna Academy, Canford Heath

The Common Question

The common question,
Left or right?
Dark or light?
Red or blue?
Cats or dogs?

But most importantly,
Christmas or Halloween?

Pumpkins or mistletoe?
Fear or joy?
Spiders or ornaments?

Maybe you're more into flesh and gore?
Or maybe you prefer a couple of gifts or more?
Either way, it's up to you,
But I prefer Easter.

Athena Shukry (13)
Magna Academy, Canford Heath

My Dark Room

Time stops as the world moves forward,
So much time and little to do.
In a big black box, I lay sterile for hours,
My eyes open and my mouth closed.
Filled by the void of loud silence,
A comfort that surrounds me like a barrier.
As I'm alone in my sedate dark room,
A calmness fills me as I feel safe.
My darkroom is my home,
And a meaningless place in space.

Lucy Moutray (12)
Magna Academy, Canford Heath

Untitled

The world is weaker
It was strong but not now
We are ruining it

We create, at the risk of destruction
We're losing animals like the black rhinos

Extinct or alive, human or not
We're all the same

I love this planet
Calm seas, lovely white clouds
Cars, planes, rockets
We're putting our world in grave danger.

Dylan Wilson (12)
Magna Academy, Canford Heath

Different

Just wish I was different
After school it's like I wear a mask
But people don't like it

Only people like you will understand
Just wish I was different
Different can be good

Just wish I was different
But it won't be the same
I wish I had more friends
Who were different like me

Just wish I was different.

Bella Churchill (13)
Magna Academy, Canford Heath

The Art Of Football

The art of football,
What can I say?
Jogo Bonito,
The beautiful game.

The World Cup,
Once every four years.
Many happy faces,
Some with tears.

Country of Brazil,
The best around.
Five World Cups,
With more inbound.

City of Liverpool,
Top of their league.
Slott ball in action,
At its peak.

Leonardo Cornachini Paiva (13)
Magna Academy, Canford Heath

Halloween

Mysterious shadows linger around every corner,
Stringy webs hanging from roof to roof.
Ghosts haunting homes,
Spiders sprawling around.
Crackling laughter like bones breaking in half,
The glowing moon illuminated the sky with cold chills.
Everyone's mind flips for one night and one night only,
It's that night of the year,
Halloween!

Lilie Walters (13)
Magna Academy, Canford Heath

Change

I remember
When I saved they cheered
When I missed they didn't jeer
They said well done
And carried on
But now
When I save no cheers
When I miss they all jee,
Why change?
What is change?
Change can be good
Change can be bad
Change can be happy
Change can be sad
Change can be *anything.*

Oliver Nippard (13)
Magna Academy, Canford Heath

Deep End

The vast ocean,
Bigger than the land.
Everything in slow motion,
But the surface area grand.

For every turtle you see,
Some people can't meet.
It could be the key,
To the food of the fleet.

Since everything dies,
There will be an end.
But we won't know what lies,
In the deep end.

William P Roberts (12)
Magna Academy, Canford Heath

Last Minutes

Last minutes,
Pressure is on now,
Thoughts fly through my head.
What if I miss?
What if I let my team down?
I get passed to,
I start to run down the wing,
The crowd roars!
Goalie jumps,
A tragic miss for the other team!
Heart pounds, ball hits the net,
I can't believe it;
I actually scored!

Hope Hatchard (13)
Magna Academy, Canford Heath

The Autumn Dream

The time I truly feel free
Autumn.
The golden, amber leaves crunching,
Beneath my feet.
The crisp morning air,
Engulfing the dark sky.
Fog clinging to windows
Looking as if it was a mirror
After a warm shower.
Spherical pumpkins carved
At every house.
It was perfect
But it was all a dream.

Julia Chudek (12)
Magna Academy, Canford Heath

I'm Human

I'm human, mistakes will be made
I try to fix them, but I can't
I'm not all-powerful
I'm not God
I cry
I fight
I love
I'm happy
I'm angry
I'm nervous
I'm disgusted
I'm embarrassed
I'm bored
I'm envious
But I'm only human.

Leon Bailey (12)
Magna Academy, Canford Heath

Sea Life

Down in the ocean,
Where the fish bloom,
Are plastic bottles,
Letting out toxic fumes.

Coral and sharks,
There are jellyfish and eels,
They're all dying,
From being reeled.

We need to be careful,
Keep our plastic away,
Since all the fish,
Will soon decay.

Lexi Roberts (13)
Magna Academy, Canford Heath

Emotions

    E njoyment - when I'm enjoying something, I smile
    M ad - when I'm mad, I get angry
    O TT - over the top
O **T** T - over the top
    I have feelings
    O TT - over the top
    N ormally - when I feel normal, I am normal
    S ad - when I'm sad, I cry.

Eva Martin (12)
Magna Academy, Canford Heath

The Beach

Look at the blue sky,
The golden sun rays,
Reflecting off the waves,
Shining like silk.
Her golden face smiles,
In wonder at the sea,
As white gulls' pale wings,
Battle the wind.
I'm stunned into silence;
My words can't capture,
The beauty of nature.

Ometh Samarasekara (13)
Magna Academy, Canford Heath

F1 With The Lads

They say that beauty is,
From the screen,
To the ring,
To the pen,
To the king,
There's always drama in F1 when we ring,
During the week I play,
Badminton, football and basketball,
In defence,
At the weekend,
I play F1,
With Jayden, Noah, Zac and Jake.

Ethan King (13)
Magna Academy, Canford Heath

Poetry

Poetry, some love poetry
Some focus mainly on poetry
You can like poetry
You can dislike poetry
But it will always stay the same
Only you can decide if you want to change poetry
You may not just change poetry
You could change the history of poetry
With just your mind.

Charlie Fitzgerald (13)
Magna Academy, Canford Heath

Hidden Truth

Roses aren't always red,
Violets aren't exactly blue,
The society that we live in,
Isn't always true

Smiles aren't always happy,
Frowns aren't always upset,
People judge too quickly,
And our feelings are what they forget.

Sophia Pritchard (13)
Magna Academy, Canford Heath

My Spotlight On Stage

On stage,
I'm under the spotlight,
Being anyone I choose.

The lights shine down on me!
The musicals are endless;
Heathers, Six, Cats, Hamilton,
You name it!
Grease, Annie, Mama Mia,
What a selection!

Ella Vincent (12)
Magna Academy, Canford Heath

World Cup

Kick and pass, score goals,
Let's play to win our country,
It's World Cup, people all around,
World sees the champion,
To give the crown
We have hope and trust in you,
Let's win it as a team.

Ometh Samarsekara (13)
Magna Academy, Canford Heath

Eagles

In the quiet of the rainforest, there's a familiar call.
It's a Philippine eagle, standing tall.
But, in all beauty, there's a truth
And there are no more eagles on the forest roof.

Paige Robins (13)
Magna Academy, Canford Heath

Sausage Rolls

Sausage rolls,
Life is tasteless without sausage rolls,
Sausage rolls, sausage rolls, sausage rolls
Dip it in ketchup all day long
I love sausage rolls.

Lewis Hill (12)
Magna Academy, Canford Heath

Piano Power

The elegancy of
The monochrome ivory,
Flows its heavenly song
Through the air.
Hundreds of ballroom dancers
Parade across the sky.

Ollie Schofield (13)
Magna Academy, Canford Heath

Untitled

Domino's,
It's so delicious,
Pineapple,
Cheese and ham,
The pizza is heavenly,
Like a tasty angel.

Mia-Lilly Pill (12)
Magna Academy, Canford Heath

Football

Down the wing
Volley header goal
In the net
Is where it goes
Game is over, we won
Victory is ours.

Aaron Hill (12)
Magna Academy, Canford Heath

Rainforest

Rebuilding animal homes to help the snakes and other rainforest animals survive
Animal charities rescue homes and lots more
I strongly believe all animals, especially reptiles
Should be cared for in all the ways possible and should all have a home to live in
No animal should be left with death
But people don't see the beauty that animals bring
And that they have feelings too
Even in the rainforest we can keep them from harm
Friends, all humans have friends and family
So why don't we help the animals
Keep them and they can have friends and family as well
Only animals have to live outside and have to hunt for food
So why can't we help all the wild animals live a longer life?
Roar, think of the song, roar
She helped the animals so the animals help her
Why can't reality be like that?
Eggs, reptiles lay eggs and birds and some other animals as well
Although, not all of them lay eggs
We can take care of them
So they need help but they don't get it
Because it could be a snake or other reptile that people are scared of
So they could become extinct and that is upsetting.
To care for an animal you need to be able to handle it and touch it

If it's a cat or a dog
It could also be any other friendly animal
But if it is a reptile or unusual animal or pet you have to be able to handle it.

Poppy Stott (11)
Matravers School, Westbury

Christmas

Christmas is almost near,
Where everyone brings Christmas cheer.
Time to put up the Christmas tree,
We are ready for Halloween to leave.

This is where we start to hang up the star,
Christmas isn't too far.
This is a time when we can snuggle down and watch Christmas movies,
Smelling the cinnamon candles is soothing.

Children playing in the snow,
This is the year to start making cookie dough.
Ripping off the wrapping paper,
Getting ready for Christmas dinner later.

Lots of kids playing with their brand-new toys,
All you can hear in the street is children making noise.
Time to snuggle down into our duvets ready,
To go to sleep and think *wow! This was the best Christmas Day ever.*

Holly Butcher (14)
Matravers School, Westbury

It's Time To Save The Survivors

These graceful creatures have roamed our seas,
For over 400 million years,
But what chance do they have,
With our presumptions and unfounded fears?

From over-fishing of our seas,
To mass pollution,
These misunderstood animals need us to find a solution,
All shark species are a vital part of the ecosystem,
The human race needs to understand,
And use their inactive, inert brains and wisdom,
Humankind are responsible for most of these shark deaths,
Leaving these defenceless sharks,
To take their final breaths.

Georgia Scott (11)
Matravers School, Westbury

Astartes

Day to day, we complete our duty, and our duty is to kill and kill until our metal boots are painted bloody.
Day to day we fight for the emperor of mankind, we fight for the sin of our people.
Day to day we await our duty as our duty is to die fighting for humanity itself.
Day to day we think about the deed we do for the most respectable end is death, for it is our duty.
Day to day we think that our existence is a shame and terror, the only peace we get is death. For we are Astartes and we shall know no fear.

Lev Dzisiak (13)
Matravers School, Westbury

The Ugly Truth

People look at their tech and see the AI of nature
But when will they stop and think is it literally like this?
When will they really stop and see the ugly truth?
From animals big and small,
All different in sizes and shapes,
Global warming is at stake from the past with sunny skies,
And green grass from the past with bright skies and clear seas.
When will they see the ugly truth?

To the present with tech and AI and networks and games,
When will they see the ugly truth?
When will you see the ugly truth with nature all around you?
But no, you look down at your phones while all around animals die and go extinct,
From bird species to spiders to mammals.
But no, you don't see the damage,
You don't care if you litter,
You don't care, you don't bother, you don't see.
Ask, look, check, you don't, you don't, you don't.

When will we all see the ugly truth?

Hadia Kawal
Pedmore High School, Stourbridge

The Truth Behind Eyes

Each day I walk in solitude,
My eyes always on him,
But I remain unnoticed,
Why would he care? All I am
Is a nobody in a world of
Isolation. I wish I had someone...

My eyes are on her. Always.
She's like pure and utter perfection,
Like a rose in a field of daisies,
A gem in a pool of stones. Perfect,
I just wish I had the courage,
The courage to tell her how I feel, how I care...

I can feel his eyes on me...
Is this happening? Finally?
No. He doesn't care... I wish he did.

Her sparkling smoky eyes on mine,
I feel like I could drown in them,
Oh, how I care about her...

Days pass, hours fly,
This is the day. I will tell her.

I told her. She smiled,
Smiled for the first time in ages.
Oh, how it brightened my day,
Like the rays of sunlight peeking through a blanket of clouds.

He does care... I was wrong.
The truth came out,
All I could do was smile,
Smile at him, smile because of him.

So he does care...

Rebeka Jurek
Pedmore High School, Stourbridge

Untitled

People are like KFC
Some are big, some are small
And if you get through the skin
You'll reach the meat
And if you go further you'll reach the bone
Some have more meat, some have less
Some may be crispy, some may be soft
You'll even have some with burnt chicken
But deep down we're all a little grumpy
But that doesn't stop us from doing what we love
But sometimes we could feel greasy
But it doesn't mean you can't be picked
But in the end, you will get picked
But even if you don't look good you will always find the one
But you will always be picked
So never give up
Always follow your bucket
And never let go of your chips
You'll never know when it's yours or their last.

Love is like KFC's gravy
You won't stop eating it
Because it's delicious
Love is like KFC's chicken
It's finger-licking good.

Ethan Cox
Pedmore High School, Stourbridge

The Beautiful Truth

Some people have nothing to do,
They have nothing to eat, no food,
They have nowhere to sleep, no bed,
They have nowhere to sit,
Not even an odd chair.
This is cruel, dreadful, and it's not fair,
But they're still grateful.

Other people have everything they need,
They have a private chef for fancy food,
They have a servant to put them to bed,
They have fancy furniture, fancy beds, fancy tables and fancy chairs,
But a lot of these people aren't grateful.
This isn't fair.

Everybody is different,
Like apples and oranges,
And pencils and peas.
Everybody is different,
Some need help,
Some don't need help,
But do what you can and just be grateful.

Deen Ahmed (12)
Pedmore High School, Stourbridge

School

School... it kinda sucks
First period is coming, oh shucks
Boring lesson... probably
unless of course it is PE

Oh no... it's PSHE
We're gonna be in the same room for eternity
Now they are getting the books out
I really, really, really wanna shout.

When will this lesson end
Teachers telling you off for messing
about with your friend
Finally this lesson's finished
Now it's time for me to vanish

Second period is Spanish
Now it is time for me to vanish
I want it to be the month of May
Can I end, this school day?

Yes it is is break,
But I'm only half awake
Gonna go to the concert too!
Hoping nothing gets on my shoe?

Because when will this lesson end
Teachers telling you off for messing about
with your friend

Finally this lesson's finished,
Now it's time for me to vanish...

Alvy Lawerence (13)
Pedmore High School, Stourbridge

Untitled

Let's talk about reality.
Some small,
Some tall,
Some mourn,
Some cry,
Some die,
Some feel alive.

Let's talk about reality,

Some talk,
Some bark,
Some none at all,
Some see,
Some bleed,
Some could even create a need.

Let's talk about reality,

Some hear,
Some are dear,
Some don't see clear,
Some can fly,
Some can sigh,
Some can even disappear!

Let's talk about reality,
Some are young,
Some are old,

Some are cold,
Some are dark,
Some are light,
Some are even clear!

Let's talk about reality.

Everyone is different,
Even me and you,
Everyone is human,
And should be treated so.
If you are reading this,
I just want to let you know
Everyone is different
And that is okay too.

Eva Brazier (11)
Pedmore High School, Stourbridge

Untitled

Palestine and Israel
Ukraine and Russia
Society...
This is society today
No more wars
No more fighting
Peace is going but we can still fight for it
Why are people dying
When we're on the couch lying?
Why don't we do something?
Why don't we stop this?
Why, why, why?
Oh wait, I know
Because we're watching a football game
While people are getting killed
Over a piece of land they don't even own
But why do they want a piece of land
Even though they have more than enough?
I don't care about a fifty-pound note
I care about a person being fed and safe enough
And if you do give me the fifty-pound note
I will give it to the person who needs it most.

Aadam Khan (12)
Pedmore High School, Stourbridge

The Show

Come on, you can do this
I breathe heavily
The spotlight glistens on me
People talking
Are they talking about me?
Oh no! I'm a freak
I freeze
My legs feel like ice
This isn't nice
Tears in my eyes
Now silence comes to rise

Step... step... step, my blood pumps to the steps
My ears ring
Oh no! I have stagefright
My heart beats like a tornado, it beats to the tune
I can't believe this is happening
Someone save me soon

Noise rises but it's like it's on max level!
The music rises to my ears
I can't breathe but I try
My feet start to beat to the rhythm of the night
A spark in me comes to life.

Maddison Bowen (11)
Pedmore High School, Stourbridge

Silenced Memories

The silence is loud,
The quietness noisy,
My pen may be writing my thoughts,
But not what I want to say,
The fullness now empty,
My ink running out,
This world we now live in has come crashing down,
And everyone is just,
It is all just silence.

The echo of bombs haunts the memory of what was,
What was happy and gleeful,
The joy was outstanding,
Now it's just a legend people think is true,
As we fake our lives, our smiles, our laughter,
We all watch our world crumble in disaster.

Silence, we all just watch in silence,
As we crumble to our knees,
The world we once loved,
Now mere memories,
And we just watch in silence.

Mya Fleming
Pedmore High School, Stourbridge

Unique

People are happy and some are sad,
Some are ambidexterity and some are not,
People are extroverted and some are not,
No matter what, everyone is unique.

People like football, however, others don't,
Some people like winter, some don't,
People like sports, but some like art,
Everyone is a unique, coloured spark in their own way.

People are multilingual and some are not,
Some like board games, some don't,
People prefer books, some don't,
Some like poems, however, some don't.

Some people are religious, some are atheist,
Some like computers, some don't,
However, everyone has their own uniquely coloured dot on humanity.

Umar Ahmed (12)
Pedmore High School, Stourbridge

Truth And Lies

Truth versus lies - people talking, gossiping, showing no mind.
Every day, in every place, there have been lurking snakes.
There is no truth; there are no lies, only criminals whom I despise.
People wearing disguises - why is the world full of truth and lies?

The nation is full of deception and betrayal,
Like monuments that are old and stale.
Some have told the truth; some have lied.
Like two things bound together in a knot that gets tied.

We do have friends; we do have rivals,
Forever mixing together in a spiral.

But in the end - will truth survive,
Or will lies thrive, keeping us blind?

Sami Abbas (14)
Pedmore High School, Stourbridge

Ideas

All emotions present one thing,
Emotional breakdown.
The yearning for attention,
Yearning for love.
All come back to one thing,

"How you feel."

The things that I did to yearn for love and attention,
All go back to dust all my efforts,
All my time to become dust.

The things I did to become famous,
To become known by all.
Crumble down to dust.
Things I did to only become a person's puppet,
For all I did, was dust.

Don't let it happen to anyone,
To anybody.
Because it hurts.
It kills a person to become a cracked-up pot,
Spools of suffering in ordered rows.

Vuyisile Bango (14)
Pedmore High School, Stourbridge

Untitled

People say, "Sticks and stones can break my bones,
And words can never hurt."
But half the time that's just a lie
And words can hurt the most.

Bones break and heal, bruises come and go,
But if something is said that you do not like,
It can keep you up all night.

When something is said that you do not like,
It doesn't feel right.
You act like it didn't hurt
But after, you feel the worst,
You feel you're not good enough,
You can't do anything right
And you feel a sinking feeling inside.

So yes, sticks and stones can break my bones,
But words hurt the most.

Jessica-Mai
Pedmore High School, Stourbridge

The Truth About Our World

The trees are green
The sky is blue
The sun is bright like fire light to a candle
The grass is green
Waving left and right
The blue ocean whistles in pain
As more plastic bags walk into the water
Skies go grey
Trees are dark
The sun gets covered by the clouds
Grass stops waving
No sunlight shines
No snow comes by Christmas
Just clouds cover the light
Plastic things get on the floor
The old sunny sun has gone
No more light, sun, snow
Just old rain and grey, sad clouds
Animals get weaker as our weather turns
No more shelter for them to go
This is the truth about our world.

Kimberley Moroua
Pedmore High School, Stourbridge

The Beautiful Truth

You are beautiful inside and out,
Don't let the world give you self-doubt,
When your head is spinning,
Remember why life is worth living,
And it'll be alright,

No one is perfect,
But no one can choose,
Who they are,
But what they do,

When your head is spinning,
Thinking self-doubt is winning,
What do you choose,
Do you win or lose?

Words above,
Saying you are not loved,

But to tell you the truth,
You are amazing,
You are the bomb,
Life can be a tragedy,
Or a sitcom,

But just remember,
It'll be alright!

Molly Wheelwright
Pedmore High School, Stourbridge

Untitled

From trees and leaves,
peas and seas,
and even cups of teas,
they are all different,
including the price of rent,
we are all not the same,
but some of us might go insane,
if you go at a single pace,
you might win the race,
but if you are last,
it's all in the past,
as long as you are being you,
even when on the loo,
so don't give up,
just do a press-up,
even if you are in a wreck
you might say, "What the heck?"
So don't think bad of yourself,
because you are better than you think,
so don't stop and be you!

Benjamin Hunt
Pedmore High School, Stourbridge

Rhythm

Music is like a city of colour.
Twists and turns.
Ebbs and flows,
Its rhythm can guide the mind
Through the mines
Of the world.

Step on the pedal
Or play a key.
Blow a hole
Or take a seat.
However your rhythm goes
It always flows.

Bongos or pans
Violas or stylos
Keyboards and pianos
Electric or acoustic.
Whatever instrument you play,
It always flows
However the rhythm goes.

Music is like a city of colour.
Twists and turns.
Ebbs and flows.
Its rhythm can guide the mind
Through the depth.

Marcy Cheslin
Pedmore High School, Stourbridge

The Grey Area

Like a shadow, I stand in the corner,
Silent as death,
Noticed by all
But accepted by none.
Is this true,
Is the world really black and white
Or is there more grey than we think?
I stand in the corner
But am I really accepted by none
Or am I in the grey area?
In the darkness of everlasting night
Your life becomes an unnecessary plight.
Look for the grey.
In life, the black is lies and
The white is truth.
But is it all truth and lies
Or do they mingle?
Do black and white and truth and lies
Mingle to make the grey?

Ethan Munjunju
Pedmore High School, Stourbridge

Being Unique

There are many people
in this world.
There's young and old.
I'm Chloe
I don't care what people think of me,
as long I'm proud to be me.
You should be too
as you're beautiful
from your toes to the very top.

I like swimming.
I enjoy sewing.
I like having fun.
My favourite colours are pink and black.
What do you like?
We're all unique.

I want to fly,
do my wildest dreams
you're beautiful,
you're unique
do whatever you desire.

Chloe Leonard
Pedmore High School, Stourbridge

Untitled

It whispers to me every night
Trying to bring me back to its frozen shores
A land of Vikings, ice and cold
Small and alone
Forgotten and afraid
This little country breathes life again
A frosty paradise
Its inky moors
Every memory
Make me want it more
Its life is cast
Reeling me in
The molten rock warms my skin

Wherever I go I see an inn
Always a place to rest
A happy country
A lovely home
Bringing me in
To myths unknown
Iceland
My sweet second home.

Thomas Bunting (13)
Pedmore High School, Stourbridge

Don't Rush Into Anything Deep

Lies, the world filled with swimming pools of lies
Don't drown yourself in them or everyone says their last goodbyes
Nobody is real
They expect you to be made of steel
Being alone crying rivers of tears
Only when you show you've had enough
Is when people open their ears
When you show yourself and take off your disguise
Everyone then flies
But why did you have to?
Your lies cutting me like a shard of glass
Why?
I miss seeing you in class
I miss you
I'm sorry.

Sophia Coleiro (13)
Pedmore High School, Stourbridge

Calming Art

Art is peace.
You start it,
You finish, calm and relaxed.
Art is fun.
Sometimes, your drawings could mean something.
Sometimes, your inspiration is a person.
Sometimes, it is an object.

A spark of creativity, and spark of peace,
Could go a long way without hurting anyone.
Sometimes, you can get annoyed at a mistake you have made,
But you can erase it and start again.
You can do pop art, macaroni art, chibi art, realism art and more.
But all art types are peaceful and fun.

Amie-Lou Owers
Pedmore High School, Stourbridge

My Classroom Poem

The clock is staring at me
I don't care about who is staring at me
I saw the chart about respect
I don't care about who bullies me
I care about respect

I don't care that school is finished
I care about learning and reading
I don't care about my pen
I care about my career

I care about my career
I don't care about what happens rarely
I don't care about who says bad things about me
I don't care about who saw me doing hard work.

Amina Bashyer
Pedmore High School, Stourbridge

Untitled

I don't have inspiration
I don't know what to write
The world is filled with voices
Telling truths and lies
Why are people like this?
The world has become a tip
Because of a tiny, pathetic rip
Why has the world become like this?
Tumbling, crumbling, ripping
I've lost all sense of hope
I've lost all my inspiration
I no longer need to write
I'm done, I'm finished
Fix this world
Make it alright
Share the beautiful truth.

Kaiya Hoskins (13)
Pedmore High School, Stourbridge

Drawing Poem

Watching the pen draw all over the paper,
Trying not to draw in a wonky line.
I drew as the birds chirped outside my window.

I love to draw for its part of my soul,
I cannot stand to live without it.
For it gives me memories of the past.

Whether it's cartoons or realistic drawings,
It helps me to focus on the important things in life.

Sometimes, it makes me wonder,
About all of the possible drawings,
that could possibly be drawn.

Thayne (11)
Pedmore High School, Stourbridge

A Cry For Peace

In lands where ancient stories tell,
A tale of sorrow hard to tell,
The echoes of conflict fill the air,
In Palestine's heart, a heavy despair,
With every tear that falls like rain,
Hope flickers dim yet still remains,
For peace is a dream we all must share,
In the midst of chaos, we must care,
Let voices unite, let hatred cease,
For in understanding, we find our peace,
Together we stand hand in hand,
To heal the wounds of this troubled land.

Shourouk Haj Ibrahim (11)
Pedmore High School, Stourbridge

Dreams

The dreams and stars
I see through my car
I find my dreams
Through the stars
The way I come
Is through my people
The people that I keep close by me
The people that I love
The people that I look up to
And the people I live with

The dreams and stars
I see through my car
By my heart I keep a space
For the people that take my taste
Many have taken
Many have not
But I am fine with that
Fine with their decision.

Muhammad Yusuf Ali-Usman (11)
Pedmore High School, Stourbridge

Dino-Nuggets

Dino-nuggets are all different
Some are nice and crispy
Others are smooth and crunchy
It's just like humans
Humans can be tall and funny
Whilst others are short and stabby.

Another reason all dino-nuggets are different
Some are burnt and black
Whilst others are white as snow
It's just like humans
Humans can be kind and happy
Others can be solemn and angry.

Everyone is like a dino-nugget
Everyone is different.

Hidayah Ilyas
Pedmore High School, Stourbridge

Is It Okay To Have Opinions?

What do you prefer?
Hot or cold?
Small or bold?
Summer or fall?
Football or basketball?
It's your opinion

What do you prefer?
Lego or Hotwheels?
Snapchat or Instagram reels?
Day or night?
Maybe you have fun with a fright?
It's your opinion

What do you prefer?
Eggs fried or boiled?
Crisps straight or coiled?
It doesn't matter because
At the end of the day
It's your opinion!

Jack Davis (12)
Pedmore High School, Stourbridge

Are You Alright?

Feelings are like a never-ending battle
You feel like you're going to lose.
But then you find a spark,
It spreads all over you like a tree and its bark.
You then see someone,
Struggling with the battle you almost lost,
Just ask, "Are you alright?"
And they will see a light,
To better days that are more bright.
One simple question is all it takes
To make someone's day great.

Lilly Skelding (13)
Pedmore High School, Stourbridge

Night Ride

The hum of the wind
The revs of an engine
Speeding down into the moonlight.
Every stop a passionate hop.
Every turn a sweet melody.
With each look they are mesmerised.
Speeding down till the end.
The lights bright powering it on.
Years and years of onlookers.
Yet no one has enough time.
Just a hobby to some,
A profession to others
An obsession to few
A collector's worth.

Lily-Ann Mills (14)
Pedmore High School, Stourbridge

Family

Dolphins swimming,
Sharks playing,
Whales somersaulting,
All together like a family,
No separation,
No fighting.
Suddenly, a net appears,
Blood, cuts and bruises,
Family or foe?
We will never know,
No longer together,
Or side by side,
Whales on show,
Dolphins endangered,
Sharks become a danger,
Fighting just for show,
No longer together,
Or side by side.

Lacey Price-Adkins
Pedmore High School, Stourbridge

Reality Of The World

Devastation
It's featured across the nations,
War, hunger, forest fires,
Burning tyres,
"I can't breathe!"
Racism is rife,
Watch out
In England, teenagers get stabbed by a knife.
So many swirling, twirling, spiralling clouds,
Can whisk you away with 1,000-knot wind.
So many lives lost,
So many lives wasted,
So many lives could've been saved.

Joshua Hedworth (14)
Pedmore High School, Stourbridge

Different

People are fat
People are skinny
People are pretty
And people are dumb
People are different
Nobody's just like you
You can call someone ugly
You can call someone dumb
But everyone's different
And so are you
Don't ruin someone's day if they smell
It's better to be nice than to be mean
Don't laugh when they fall
Everybody is different.

Grace Peters (12)
Pedmore High School, Stourbridge

Animals Are Cool

Animals can fly,
Such as pigeons, dogs and cats.
No, dogs and cats can't.
But who says you can't imagine it?

Think about being an animal that can fly,
A bird, an owl, there are many.
Imagine you are flying around and you find your prey,
You go to attack it and swing it around like a dog with a sack.

Only to find your prey is a rock.

Eduard Baloi (12)
Pedmore High School, Stourbridge

Voice

Your voice is a choice.
A choice taken by most.
Like butter on toast.
A voice is given to the ones who have power.
Those who wish to be heard, seem absurd.
But it is an endless battle.
And it is won by only the ones who fight.
Like how suffragettes suffered to be heard.
And speak their word.
So will you, but always know it's worth it.

Eddie Lewis Bladen
Pedmore High School, Stourbridge

Bullying

Imagine a bully as a door hinge,
Now imagine an orange between the door and the door hinge,
You are the orange,
Bullies will crush you down if you let them,
While they crush they will break your core,
They will beat you until you tell someone,
If you don't your mental health will severely decrease,
Don't let them bring you down.

Daniel Davis (14)
Pedmore High School, Stourbridge

Challenges

C oping with school,
H omework being hard,
A rguments with friends and family,
L ying to parents,
L eaving friends,
E nergy,
N agging sister,
G rowing up,
E ating,
S creaming, shouting and crying.

Isabella Davies (12)
Pedmore High School, Stourbridge

Art

What are your favourite things?
Is it arts and crafts
Or a nice warm bubble bath?
Are you tall or short?
Do you like a certain sport?
What does a good friendship mean to you?
Do you like going to the zoo?
Anyway love what you do
Because it is specific to you.

Theo Darnley (11)
Pedmore High School, Stourbridge

Who Am I?

I am smart,
I am ugly,
I am normal,
I am weird,
I am me,

I am artistic,
I am sporty,
I am fat,
I am thin,
I am human,

Some people think I am crazy,
While others may think I am fine,
But what do I think?
Who am I?

Coralie Jones (12)
Pedmore High School, Stourbridge

Bubbles

Big foamy bubbles
Big clear bubbles
Bubbles in my bath
Bubbles in my sink
Bubbles made from soap
Bubbles on my dog
Being eaten by a hog
Bubbles in my hair
Being worn by a bear
Bubbles blown from wounds
Bubbles in ink, filling the sink.

Scarlett Homer (11)
Pedmore High School, Stourbridge

Music

When the beat of the drum hits
I feel it in my body
When the tweet of the flute hits
I feel it in my mind
When the honk of the tenor horn hits
I feel it in my heart
And when I feel the rhythm
I feel it in the blood pumping through my veins.

Anastasia Archer-Smith
Pedmore High School, Stourbridge

The Mind Of A Rock

The water flows
Down the stream
Across the rivers
And through an open stream
The rock goes up and down
Side to side
And upside down
Someone grabs it and swings it round
And round
Let's go and run around.

Saif Asghar (12)
Pedmore High School, Stourbridge

My Emotions

Sometimes emotions can take over us like anger
But we need to know we should calm down and reset
It might be that sadness can start to creep in
And we might need time for ourselves
Joy could fill us and we could be happy.

Kai Toogood
Pedmore High School, Stourbridge

Sexism

S ome girls can't vote
E xtreme things happen
e **X** treme views on men
I n some countries women can't work
S exist people around the world
M ales are first-class citizens.

Natalia Fetita (13)
Pedmore High School, Stourbridge

Sleep

Having a nightmare and you get to the end when it's all a dream,
Then you wake up and scream,
Lying on my bed makes me feel like I'm on a cloud,
And it makes me never want to get out.

Tuliyah-Jae Sutton
Pedmore High School, Stourbridge

Theatre

Behind the scenes is never what it seems
Acting on stage can be very strange in a way
The audience is staring
With all the lights blaring
I step onto the stage.

Imogen Harris (11)
Pedmore High School, Stourbridge

Respect

R espect
E veryone matters
S how kindness
P oliteness
E mpathetic
C hoose respect
T ake responsibility.

Aisha Ahmed (12)
Pedmore High School, Stourbridge

Rainbow

You called me your rainbow,
Long, long ago, I was your rainbow,
But when I found my rainbow,
It was in a sky full of clouds,

And I fell from my colours,
A world of inky black falling past,
I turned my world to poison with its anger.

Words, endless words,
They spun and spiralled,
Painting the truth that I hid,
That we'd hid,
In a beautiful arc across the sky,
A shifting, shaping beauty.

Falling faster through the sky,
Grasping, clutching, screaming,
Everything blurred past.

Too proud to call for help,
The sky turned as red as my loathing,
My frothing, foaming loathing,
For what I was.

Fleeing, hurling, sprinting from your painted truth,
From your revealed colours,
From your loving words.

Hating words,
Hating, loving,
Hating because you told,
Loving because you cared,
Hating, loving,
Crying.

You freed me, you killed me,
You saved me,
For when I clutched again,
At the clouds,
The once harsh, cruel clouds,
They held me up,
Strong with their colours,
With my colours,
With our colours,

And I watered the ground,
With my tears,
As I sat on my rainbow with you.

Eve Tiddeman (12)
Penglais School, Aberystwyth

Beautiful Truth

B oldly speaking with a heart so pure,
E mpathy grows like a blossoming flower,
A llowing honesty to light the way,
U nderstanding blooms like dawn's first ray,
T rust takes root, a tree sits strong,
I nspiring connections, harmonising along,
F orging bonds in daylight's hue,
U nfolding strength, sincere and true,
L ove and integrity shining through.

T he essence of truth, a guiding star,
R adiates beauty, near and far,
U nveils the depths of the human soul,
T akes courage, making hearts whole,
H ow beautiful, how beautiful the truth can be.

Rhiannon Starr (11)
Penglais School, Aberystwyth

Summer, Autumn, Winter And Spring

Summer is warm and the sun shines bright
Ice cream on the beach, swimming and playing
Sand mermaids and ginormous sandcastles

Crispy leaves and darker nights
Brown trees and different sights
Scary costumes and lit pumpkins

Snow is falling and people are coming
Carols are being sung and decorations are being hung
It's the time of giving so give me a ho-ho-ho

Baby animals are being born and all the trees are shooting leaves
The sun starts to come up earlier and all the flowers come to play
But in-between the rain and the sun and the nights and the days
There always is time for fun.

Tilly Greenhalgh-Donnai (11)
Penglais School, Aberystwyth

October, October

October, October,
Your colourful crunchy leaves,
Makes my spine tingle,
And makes me freeze.

An autumn afternoon,
Makes me freeze,
Like I'm on the top of Mount Everest,
In a breeze.

Your festive animals,
Foxes and owls,
Squirrels and robins,
So cute I could squeal.

October, October,
Your beautiful colours,
Red, orange and yellow,
Green, purple and brown,
Pretty colours in a pretty autumn.

This shows,
How beautiful autumn is,
With its animals,
Colours and crunchy leaves.

Nancy Sophia Gorman (12)
Penglais School, Aberystwyth

Freedom

F reedom of an individual is more important than one thinks,
R ight to freedom belongs to all, no matter who it is.
E veryone is curious. But too much of anything is always bad.
E veryone has their freedom, just don't let anyone take it away.
D oing what you want is not freedom, there is more to it than that
O ur freedom is only ours and no one has the right to take it away.
M ost people think freedom is a ticket to do what we want but there is more.

Jewel Mathew (14)
Penglais School, Aberystwyth

Hot Chocolate

Hot, so hot,
Silky, creamy, sweet hot chocolate,
Sliding down my throat.
Hot chocolate always reminds me of winter.
My trough is filled with delightful flavours,
Marshmallows, pink and white.
Like snow melting in the cream.
My hands firmly in control of my mug,
But I went for the last sip,
But it's gone!

Gabriel Brown (11)
Penglais School, Aberystwyth

Truth

T ruth is a secret
R unning away doesn't do anything
U nconsciously doesn't do anything
T ruth is what keeps us apart
H esitant is alright

H arm is done
U nloved is just a word
R emember
T ruth
S cars us.

Lily Potts (11)
Penglais School, Aberystwyth

YOUNG WRITERS INFORMATION

We hope you have enjoyed reading this book – and that you will continue to in the coming years.

If you're the parent or family member of an enthusiastic poet or story writer, do visit our website **www.youngwriters.co.uk/subscribe** and sign up to receive news, competitions, writing challenges and tips, activities and much, much more! There's lots to keep budding writers motivated!

If you would like to order further copies of this book, or any of our other titles, then please give us a call or order via your online account.

Young Writers
Remus House
Coltsfoot Drive
Peterborough
PE2 9BF
(01733) 890066
info@youngwriters.co.uk

**Join in the conversation!
Tips, news, giveaways and much more!**

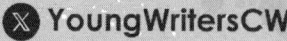

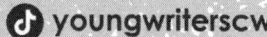